Thresher Sharks

by Jody S. Rake

CAPSTONE PRESS
a capstone imprint

Pebble Plus is published by Capstone Press,
1710 Roe Crest Drive, North Mankato, Minnesota 56003
www.capstonepub.com

Library of Congress Cataloging-in-Publication Data
Names: Rake, Jody Sullivan, author.
Title: Thresher sharks : a 4D book / by Jody S. Rake.
Description: North Mankato, Minnesota : Capstone Press,
[2019] | Series: Pebble plus. All about sharks | Audience:
Age 4–7. | Includes bibliographical references and index.
Identifiers: LCCN 2018002873 (print) | LCCN 2018008477
(ebook) | ISBN 9781977101648 (eBook PDF) |
ISBN 9781977101563 (hardcover) | ISBN 9781977101600
(paperback)
Subjects: LCSH: Alopiidae—Juvenile literature.
Classification: LCC QL638.95.A4 (ebook) |
LCC QL638.95.A4 R35 2019 (print) | DDC 597.3—dc23
LC record available at https://lccn.loc.gov/2018002873

Editorial Credits
Marissa Kirkman, editor; Charmaine Whitman, designer;
Kelly Garvin, media researcher; Kathy McColley, production
specialist

Image Credits
Alamy: imageBroker, 5, Jeff Rotman, 17; Nature Picture
Library/Doug Perrine, 19; Newscom: Paulo de Oliveira/
NHPA/Photoshot, 13, Steve De Neef Visual&Written, 15;
Shutterstock: bearacreative, 1, Maquiladora, 8, Rich Carey,
3, 24, Willyam Bradbury, 23; Superstock: Norbert Probst/
imageBROKER, cover, 7, 9, 11, 21

Note to Parents and Teachers

The All About Sharks set supports national curriculum standards for science related to the
characteristics and behavior of animals. This book describes and illustrates thresher sharks. The
images support early readers in understanding the text. The repetition of words and phrases helps
early readers learn new words. This book also introduces early readers to subject-specific vocabulary
words, which are defined in the Glossary section. Early readers may need assistance to read some
words and to use the Table of Contents, Glossary, Read More, Internet Sites, Critical Thinking
Questions, and Index sections of the book.

Table of Contents

A Surprise Attack

A hungry shark circles a huge school of fish. The shark's long tail flips as fast as lightning. Snap! A fish is stunned by the tail whip. The shark grabs its meal.

Thresher sharks can be found
in warm and cool waters.
They don't go to polar waters.
They swim both near the shore
and in the deep sea.

A Long Tail

The thresher shark is easy to spot.
Its upper tail fin is as long as its body.
It looks like a ribbon. The lower
tail fin is much smaller.

5 feet (1.5 meters)

18–20 feet (5.5 to 6 meters)

Thresher sharks are gray-blue on their backs. On their sides the color lightens to gray. Their bellies are white.

Fishing with a Whip

Thresher sharks eat small fishes. They prey on fish such as mackerel, herring, and sardines. The thresher shark hunts alone. It looks for schools of fishes.

A thresher shark uses its tail like a whip. It flips its tail over its head and into a school of fish. The tail whip hits a fish. It stops swimming. Then the shark can catch it.

Thresher sharks have small mouths. Their teeth are small, sharp, and pointy. Thresher sharks only have about 80 teeth. Other sharks may have thousands.

Thresher Shark Pups

Thresher shark pups hatch from eggs inside their mother after nine months. Two to four pups are born at a time. Thresher pups are big. They are 4 to 5 feet (1.2 to 1.6 meters) at birth.

Young thresher sharks stay near the shore. When they are grown, they head for open water. Thresher sharks become adults in about three to six years. They may live 18 to 50 years.

Glossary

hatch—to break out of an egg

mackerel—a small fish that lives in the North Atlantic Ocean

prey—an animal hunted by another animal for food

pup—a young shark

school—a large number of the same kind of fish swimming and feeding together

shore—the part of the ocean where the water ends and the land begins

stun—to shock, overwhelm, or knock unconscious

whip—to move something quickly and forcefully

Read More

Discovery Channel. *Sharkopedia: The Complete Guide to Everything Shark.* Des Moines, Iowa: Time Home Entertainment, 2014.

Ellwood, Nancy and Parrish, Margaret. *Sharkpedia.* Second Edition. New York: DK Publishing, 2017.

Meister, Cari. *Sharks.* Life under the Sea. Minneapolis: Jump!, 2014.

Internet Sites

FactHound offers a safe, fun way to find Internet sites related to this book. All of the sites on FactHound have been researched by our staff.

Here's all you do:

Visit *www.facthound.com*

Type in this code: 9781977101563

 Check out projects, games and lots more at **www.capstonekids.com**

Critical Thinking Questions

1. Describe two body parts of a thresher shark.

2. How do thresher sharks catch their prey?

3. Name a kind of prey that thresher sharks eat.

Index